A Sacred Isla

CU00402791

Iron Age, Roman a
Temples and Ritual on Hayling Island

"Among the islands that lie just off the coast of Britain are many scattered and deserted islands. Some of these are called by the names of spirits and heroes. [Demetrius] himself, by the emperor's order, had made a voyage for inquiry and observation to the nearest of these islands, which had only a few inhabitants, holy men who were all held inviolate by the Britons" (Plutarch, *Moralia* 419E)

We shall never know which island Plutarch was referring to, nor how accurate his source of information, but this brief reference to religion in pre-Roman Britain paints a vivid picture of the importance of sacred islands, of which Hayling Island, as we shall see, was one.

Introduction

Hayling Island lies within the extensive Portsmouth-Langstone-Chichester Harbour area, on the south coast of England (Fig. 1). It is a drowned landscape, and there is good evidence of geological sinking and the inundation of low-lying areas from the end of the last Ice Age onwards.[1] By the end of the Iron Age, when the first temple was built, Hayling was an island, perhaps with extensive salt marsh and mud-flats separating it from the mainland at Langstone. The exploitation of salt was an important activity on the island at this time, and may have been one of the reasons why a temple site developed here.[2] Salt-working would have been a seasonal activity, during the summer, and pilgrimages to the temple site may have been organized to coincide with this, in part to celebrate the winning of a vital commodity for the community. There were other, more political reasons for the Hayling temple, too, connected with the Iron Age tribe of the Atrebates and its royal dynasty, as we discuss in more detail below.

A Sacred Island

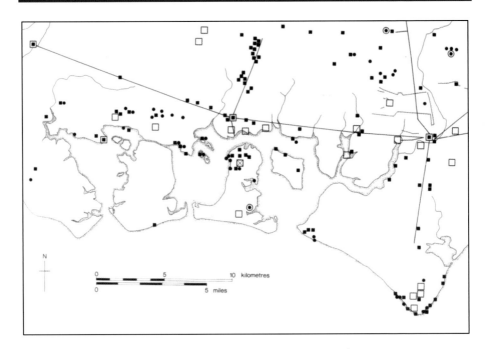

Fig. 1 *South-east Hampshire and west Sussex in the 1st century AD. Hayling Island temple is marked with a square and diagonal cross; Iron Age sites with a black dot; 1st-century Roman sites with an open square; other Roman sites with a small black square; Roman towns and forts with a larger black/open square.*

The temple site is in the middle of farmland in the northern part of Hayling Island. The whole of Hayling is very flat, and part of the coastal plain, but the temple itself was constructed on a slight, but obvious rise in the landscape, at 17 feet (5.2 m) above sea-level. In the Roman period, when the temple had a tower-like appearance, it would have been visible from many miles away, particular for travellers along the Roman road between Chichester and Winchester or Bitterne.

Excavation and fieldwork on the temple site, by the Hayling Island Excavation Project, ran for five years from 1976, after a campaign of air photography which coincided with the severe drought of that summer.[3] The site has proved to be exceptional: beneath a large Roman temple lay two successive late Iron Age timber shrines. Although there are slight traces of earlier Iron Age predecessors to many 'Romano-Celtic' temples in north-west Europe, this is undoubtedly the best example so far discovered in Britain. Dating from the early/mid 1st century BC, the Iron Age temple continued up to and beyond the Roman conquest in AD 43, being replaced on the same site by the large stone-built Roman temple in the 60s/70s AD, which mirrors the plan of the earlier shrine. Such an early date after the Roman conquest means that Hayling Island was one of the first major temples to be established in the new Roman province. It can be linked to the royal house of the Atrebates and Regni, notably to king Togidubnus, who was the probable owner of Fishbourne Palace. Excavation and post-excavation work has continued since the 1980s, and in 2000/01 a magnetometer survey and excavation revealed a fascinating and enigmatic Saxon phase of ritual activity, just to the south of the main temple site.

The First Iron Age Temple

The main feature in the Iron Age is the temple site itself, which we have divided into two major phases: the first and second Iron Age temples (Fig. 2). The first temple was built in wood in the early to mid-first century BC, and there were three main elements: an enclosure (c. 25 x 25 m) with its entrance aligned to the east, an inner enclosure, also with an eastern entrance, and a pit set on the western margin of the inner enclosure. It was probably an open-air sanctuary.

The outer enclosure was defined by a narrow square-shaped slot that was widened at intervals by semicircular post-holes. This only survived in good condition just to the south of the entrance where it had not been destroyed by the enclosure ditch of the later Iron Age temple. In form, it was probably a fence of upright posts with planking or wattles in between. There are indications that the enclosure had a double or multiple boundary, as reflected in the parallel traces of ditches for part of the boundary.

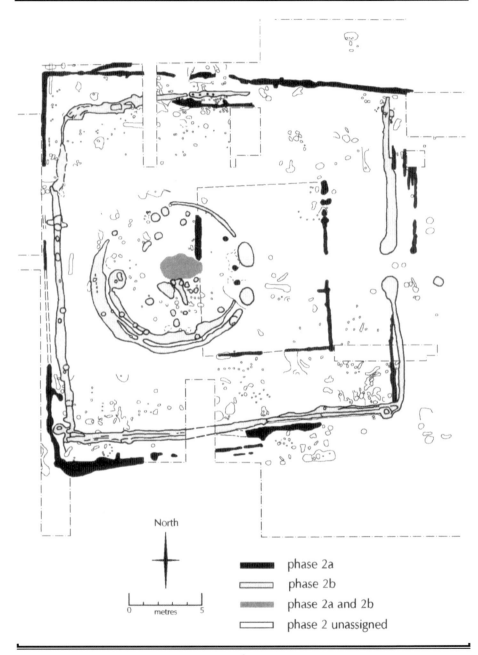

North

phase 2a	
phase 2b	
phase 2a and 2b	
phase 2 unassigned	

0 metres 5

Fig. 2 (opposite) Plan of the Iron temple. The first temple is shown in black as phase 2a, and the second temple is shown in light grey as phase 2b.

The inner enclosure was much better preserved, taking the form of a deep slot with preserved plank impressions in places, and substantial square post-holes at the corners and at intervals to support what must have been a plank-built fence. It was best preserved on its southern and eastern sides, showing clear evidence for an inturned entrance in the middle of the eastern side. Because of later structures little survived of the western side, except for a shallow beam slot to the north of the pit that interrupted the alignment on this side.[4]

The pit (Fig. 3) appears to have been an integral part of this phase, since the entrances appear to have been aligned on it, and the beam-slot referred to above respects its position. It was c. 2.5 x 1.7 m, and 0.65 m deep, but since the fill dates to the later Iron Age phase, it is possible that the pit could have been smaller in its first phase, but subsequently enlarged.

Fig. 3 The pit (shown in dark grey on Fig. 2) formed a focal point on the east side of the first temple and continued as the centre of the second temple. It contained many offerings: brooches, coins and other objects of the very Late Iron Age.

A few of the other interior features can be tentatively assigned to this phase. Two post-holes containing the charred remains of squared posts were positioned c. 2.5 m to the east of the pit. They are earlier than the entrance post-holes of the second temple's circular structure, and may have formed an element that defined the approach or surrounds of the pit. Intriguingly, a radiocarbon date from one of the post-holes gives an early date of 410-110 BC.[5] This is somewhat earlier than most of the artefacts from the site, and implies that old timbers were used.

The date of the first temple is best established from the stratified coins, since the pottery is not specific enough to help with dating the establishment of the site. The coins from this phase can all be dated to the early-mid 1st century BC, up to the 30s BC, and suggest that the first temple can be placed in the mid 1st century BC or a little later. There are some finds of 'saucepan' pottery and iron 'currency bars' that relate back to the later part of the Middle Iron Age (3rd-early 1st century BC), but none of the structures appear to be this early, with the exception of the radiocarbon date from the post-holes mentioned above.

The Second Iron Age Temple

The second temple transformed the appearance of the shrine, and made it look much more like a building than an open-air place of worship. It used the same outer enclosure, but the inner enclosure was demolished to make way for a circular building around the central pit (Fig. 4). The circular structure is made up of an inner gully, 9.2 m in diameter, with post-holes within it, presumably forming the foundation of the walling, and an outer gully of variable depth that appears to have served to drain water away from the structure's foundations. Both these features were better preserved on the south side of the circle. On the east side, the gullies terminated in post-holes forming the entrance into the structure. This seems to have been a simple, slightly projecting porch forming an entrance of c. 2.8 m, although it should be noted that the construction of the Roman temple over it may have truncated any eastward-projecting extension to the entrance. In the interior of the structure, post-holes were set out in a loosely shaped arc around the south, west and north sides, and probably served to support the roof.

To all intents and purposes, this structure is a typical round-house, of the general type known from many Iron Age sites in southern Britain, as can be seen reconstructed experimentally at Butser Ancient Farm. Architecturally, nothing distinguishes it from a domestic structure, and it can best be considered as a house for the deity, of a type that would have been familiar to inhabitants of the region in a secular context (Fig. 5).

A Sacred Island

Fig. 4 View of the second Iron Age temple's circular gullies, and the central pit. Surrounding the Iron Age features, the stone walling of the Roman cella can be seen. The photo is taken from the north-west, so the entrance to both the second Iron Age and the Roman temples is positioned on the upper left side (i.e. aligned to the east).

What served to differentiate it from a primarily domestic building, however, is the central pit, which continued in use, and the votive deposits, which also continued to be placed in the courtyard around the structure (see below). The pit and a linked feature yielded radiocarbon dates of AD 20-330, a wide date-range, but compatible with the pit and second temple continuing in use up until the construction of the Roman temple, and the covering of the pit with a paved floor, in the 60s or 70s AD.[6]

The outer boundary of the courtyard was also reorganised in this phase, resulting in a deeper, more clearly aligned ditch, particularly on the east, south and west sides. The eastern entrance is of some interest, since the ends of the ditches are slightly incurved, and in the case of the southern ditch-end, also significantly deeper than the ditch itself. Excavation indicated that this had a flat rectangular bottom (c. 0.80 x 0.40 m) that may in fact not have been a sump, as might be expected, but the bottom of a post- or stone-hole. The ditch-end had a primary fill that lined the sides, in the manner of a post or stone packing, and a later layer (dated c. AD 50/60) that filled the central part of the feature, after the post or stone had been removed. A complete rotary quernstone was found in the later layer.

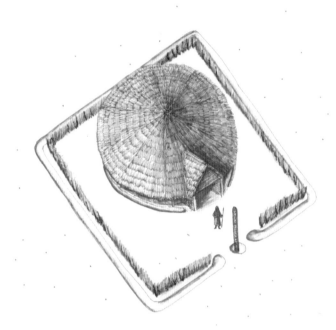

Fig. 5 Simplified reconstruction of the second Iron Age temple. It is shown as a round-house, but may have been much more highly decorated than given here. A wooden post is shown in the entrance, but a preferable alternative is a sarsen stone (see text). Drawing by Robert Downey.

The interpretation of the southern ditch-end favours the notion that it contained an upright stone that served as a marker for the entrance to the temple. Support for this comes from the finding of large rectangular sarsen boulders in the foundations of the entrance porch to the Roman temple courtyard, indicating that large stones were available and indeed were not uncommon in the region, to judge from the results of a survey of sarsen stones in Hampshire. It is possible, but unfortunately not provable, that the sarsen boulders in the Roman foundations were derived from the Iron Age phase, and had been deliberately incorporated in the structure of the Roman temple. An additional factor in favour of this interpretation is that standing stones are known to have been in use in the Iron Age, principally in Gaul.[7] A Romano-Celtic temple constructed around a standing stone is known at Triguères (Loiret).

A Sacred Island

Dating of the second temple is determined mainly by the coins. The Iron Age coinage shows an apparent gap in the early 1st century AD (see below), and this may coincide with the transition from the first to the second temples. Indeed, it is possible that the temple declined in use for a short period, but following the construction of the circular building in the early decades of the 1st century AD, activity picked up and continued to the construction of the Roman temple in the 60s AD. The coins reflect this, with a higher percentage of coins from the decades leading up to the Roman conquest. It is quite likely that Iron Age coins continued to be deposited up to the time of the construction of the Roman temple, and indeed possibly beyond, to judge from the high percentage of late Iron Age coinage associated with the Roman temple.

Finds from the Iron Age Temples

The objects deposited include a large number of coins, mainly Celtic coins of the immediate area, but also those of the peoples to the west and a significant number from Gaul, primarily from Armorica (modern Brittany) and central/northern Gaul (Fig. 6). There are also some Roman republican coins, unusual for a British Iron Age site. Study of the coins shows that they are relatively early in date, the majority being of the mid/late 1st century BC, and there may have been a gap in the practice of coin deposition in the early 1st century AD.[8] A significant feature of the coin assemblage is the high percentage of plated coins (78% of the gold and 46% of the silver coins) (Fig. 7). This is argued to be a deliberate element of ritual practice, and appears to reflect the selection of plated coins for deposition at the temple. Presumably these must be irregular issues or coins deliberately manufactured as 'temple money' to save valuable precious metal. As a rider to this, it can be suggested that the percentage of solid gold and silver coins may originally have been higher, if these were selectively positioned in or on the (second) temple structure (together with other valuable votive offerings). If so, it is unlikely that they would have been incorporated into the excavated deposits, but would have been removed during or after the construction and use of the Roman temple.

Fig. 6 Bronze coin of the Coriosolites (modern Brittany), dated to the mid-1st century BC. It shows the head of a god with a chain emerging from his forehead, attached to a human head. From a feature linked to the central pit.

Fig. 7 Plated gold coin of 'British QA' type, a predecessor to the inscribed coinage of Commius. From the circular shrine of the second Iron Age temple.

Other votive material from the site includes at least two iron 'currency bars', brooches, shield binding, iron spearheads and knives, a sword scabbard, vehicle fittings and some fragmentary human remains. The horse and vehicle equipment from both Iron Age phases includes a three-link bridle-bit of cast bronze with bronze-cased iron rein-rings, datable to the 1st century BC.[9] A terret (guide for the reins on a chariot or wagon) was also found and is probably of similar date.[10] One of the more remarkable objects found was a bronze yoke-terminal with inlaid red enamel decoration on its terminal knob. It is without parallel in Britain, but is almost identical to examples from Mont-Beuvray in central France.[11] There are several iron linch-pins, and two iron nave-hoops (for the hub of the wheel) of a type found in the Yorkshire and Champagne Iron Age vehicle burials and also at the sacred pool at Llyn Cerrig

Bach, Anglesey.[12] A number of bronze and iron rings from the site may also have been horse or vehicle trappings, or from a warrior's equipment, as at nearby Owslebury, but there is also the possibility that they are specially manufactured votive objects, such as has been suggested for those from Uley temple, Gloucestershire, and elsewhere.[13]

The martial equipment forms another important category of deposit on the temple site, and is also a characteristic of other Iron Age ritual sites in Britain and Gaul.[14] It includes a group of iron socketed spearheads, and numerous fragments of edge binding and terminal knobs for shields, similar to those from the contemporary temple site at Gournay in northern France.[15] Several pieces of body armour in the form of an iron mail tunic were an unusual find, only recovered elsewhere from wealthy Late Iron Age burial sites, such as the vehicle burial at Kirkburn, Yorkshire, and the princely grave at Folly Lane, *Verulamium*.[16] Three belt-hooks for baldrics were found, of which one winged example is only the second of its type to be found in Britain. The other example comes from the Owslebury 'warrior' burial, and both are probably continental imports.

The votive deposits contained a number of beads of glass, amber and other materials. Most of the decorated coloured glass beads were not from necklaces, but were large individual items, made in Britain or on the Continent. One originates from the Crimea (northern Black Sea area) and another is probably from eastern Europe, later embellished in Ireland, before being brought to the temple. Several of the beads had been ritually 'killed' by being broken in half.

Another significant class of find is the flintwork. Mostly it consists of scrapers of Neolithic/Bronze Age type which appear to have been deliberately deposited with the other artefacts. There is no sign that the site had pre-Iron Age activity that was disturbed and redeposited. Also of probable significance in this respect are a Neolithic polished flint axe and a Mesolithic axe from the topsoil over the temple. Although less well stratified, these can probably be linked with the practice observed at Romano-Celtic temple sites of depositing axe-heads and other much earlier artefacts.[17] Of additional relevance in this respect is the broken Middle Bronze Age spearhead from the northern post-hole of the entrance to the second temple structure. It seems likely that objects from earlier prehistory, perhaps found casually during the Iron Age as a result of activity that disturbed earlier material, were brought to the temple as votive offerings.

Human Bones: Animal Sacrifices

The small number of human bones from the temple, consisting of parts of a cranium (Fig. 8), a mandible and broken limb bones from one or more young adults, obviously raises the vexed issue of whether or not they represent human sacrifice. This practice is associated with Celtic religion in ancient literature, and there are apparent remains of victims at Gournay, Ribemont and Fesques, all three being large temples and possible 'war-trophy' sites in northern France.[18] The Hayling Island remains are too fragmentary to contribute significantly to this debate, since no forensic evidence of deliberate chopping or killing was visible on the bones, nor were their depositional positions unusual or suggestive of sacrifice. There are two points to note: firstly, the bones are amongst the general assemblage of votive offerings in the temple area and as such probably represent votive offerings, and secondly, the scattered and broken nature of the bones indicates either the deposition of disarticulated (perhaps quite old) bones as offerings, or the disturbance or a burial or human corpse within the temple area. Whether that burial resulted from a sacrifice is entirely unknown. Unfortunately the number of bones is too small to detect selection of parts of the body, as observed so dramatically at Ribemont.

Fig. 8 Top part of a human cranium, from the outer enclosure ditch of the second Iron Age temple, at its south-west corner.

The animal bones from the Iron Age phases are of some interest in that they show an almost complete lack of cattle bones, with only a handful of specimens being noted, mainly from zones outside the temple enclosure. Sheep and pig bones were almost exclusively found, with sheep predominating in terms of the number of fragments. This degree of selectivity in the assemblage is also seen at other religious sites, such as Uley where goat and chicken are predominant, and is usually assumed to be a result of selection of animals for sacrifice according to the rituals of the cult being worshipped. At Hayling Island, sheep and pig were apparently the two species regarded as worthy for votive offerings.[19]

The parts of the animals found were also noteworthy: it is possible that the better cuts of meat were offered as sacrifices to the deity, as well as parts of the skulls. The poorer cuts of meat were probably consumed by those making the offerings, and the bones disposed of elsewhere.

Deposition and Ritual in the Iron Age

Deposition within the site was primarily within the outer courtyard area, and showed a marked bias towards the south-eastern sector, i.e. on the left-hand side as worshippers came within the entrance of the temple area. This was very probably the result of the ritual used for disposing of votive offerings. It must, however, be acknowledged that the northern part of the enclosure appears to have been truncated during the construction of the Roman temple, probably in an attempt to level the ground surface. This has resulted in some of the features being relatively shallow on the north side of the second temple's circular structure and in the enclosure area to its north. Having taken this into account, it still seems that deposition in the south-east sector was a real phenomenon of Iron Age practice, since enough survived over the whole of the Iron Age temple area to demonstrate this.

Several classes of artefact show this spatial zonation. The coins (Fig. 9) tend to be clustered near the entrance to the outer enclosure, between the first temple's outer and inner enclosures and in features associated with the second temple's circular structure. Amongst these are a couple of Roman republican coins from the circular structure (but otherwise no Roman coins in this phase within the enclosure as a whole) and a 'hoard' of four coins of the Carnutes (north-central France) and two of the Aulerci Eburovices (northern France), dated to the mid 1st century BC, found together in a deposit within the south-east corner of the first temple inner enclosure.[20]

Brooches, items of personal adornment and other bronze objects such as rings and edge binding are from approximately the same locations as the coins, except in the case of the second temple circular structure, where they tend to be found in the central pit rather than the circular gullies. The pit had pieces of bracelet, rings, brooches, parts of a mirror and other dress items, which probably had deliberate votive significance, relevant in particular to the period when the pit was infilled towards the end of the Iron Age. Another concentration of bronze brooches was located next to a mudstone block (an altar?), near the entrance to the outer enclosure.[21]

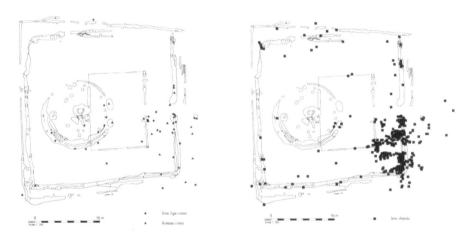

Fig. 9 Distribution of (left) coins and (right) iron objects, showing the south-east bias in the deposition of the artefacts within the temple area.

The iron-work (Fig. 9) clearly demonstrates that the south-east part of the outer enclosure, particularly on its eastern margin, was considered a focus for deposition. Most of the iron objects are small unidentifiable fragments, but of significance are nails (associated probably with wooden artefacts now decayed) and the spear-heads and knives mentioned above. The human bone is located adjacent to the south-east and south-west corners of the outer enclosure and also in the main south-eastern deposition zone within the enclosure.

Another significant practice on the site was that many of the objects were deliberately broken or bent, including several of the coins, and in addition, spearheads were often reused or sub-standard. The action of breaking or bending artefacts can be interpreted as indicating that the objects were 'killed' in an act of dedication to the deity by rendering them useless.[22] Whether or not this is the most appropriate explanation, it is clear that the high concentration of artefacts of many different classes indicates that objects, pottery vessels and animals were brought to the site, 'sacrificed' in some form to the deity, and the physical remains left as votive offerings. These offerings appear to have been regarded as inviolate,[23] and were left in and around specific locations in the temple enclosure, to be disturbed and redeposited again and again in subsequent acts of votive deposition.

The Importance of the Iron Age Temple

There are significant links with Gaul (modern France) during the Roman phase, particularly in the architectural form of the temple, as discussed later in this booklet. It is most likely that these cross-Channel links originated in the Iron Age. The temple shows many points in common with northern French temples, such as Gournay, in terms of the overall sequence, and was probably constructed as a result of the so-called Belgic influence on Britain in the first century BC.[24] We should also mention the reference by Julius Caesar to the flight of Commius, king of the northern Gaulish people of the Atrebates, to Britain in *c.* 50 BC, and the probable geographical location of this event in the Chichester/Portsmouth area.[25] In addition, Barry Cunliffe makes a case for the Belgae attested in the Winchester area in the Roman period to be a genuine reflection of a pre-Roman situation.[26] Thus, there is a possible context for the importation of religious ideas, including those concerning temple construction, alongside political and other influences flowing into central southern Britain during the Late Iron Age. The first temple was probably set up at this time and indeed indicates a more continental style in its constructional methods than the succeeding second temple structures.[27]

The first Iron Age temple appears to have been on a new site, and we do not know why this location was chosen. There are some clues: the site is on an island, a factor mentioned by ancient authors as significant;[28] it is on the highest point of the northern part of the island and would have been clearly visible from the mainland (assuming that the surrounding areas had been cleared of woodland, as seems likely); and it is close to the presumed *oppidum* (tribal centre) in the Chichester/Fishbourne area.[29] It is therefore in a privileged location relative to both the physical geography of the region and the presumed tribal focus of power at that time.

Who was it dedicated to?

The votive material from the site, especially the martial equipment and vehicle remains, has parallels in the pre-Roman phases of some of the western Gallic temples, as well as Gournay. This can be linked with the existence of a Roman inscription to Mars Mullo at the temple of Allonnes (Sarthe), to suggest that the Hayling Island Iron Age temple was dedicated to a Celtic Mars-type deity.[30] This line of argument, advanced at the time of the excavation of the temple, can be supplemented by more recent discoveries and suggestions. These focus upon the excavation of a high-status princely burial at Folly Lane, St Albans (ancient *Verulamium*), that was succeeded by a Romano-Celtic temple.[31] This sequence, combined with evidence from other sites, can be used to suggest that there were Iron Age temples (and their Romano-Celtic successors) dedicated to ancestral cults or to gods linked to hero/ancestor worship, forming a significant feature of the religious life of the period.[32]

This interpretation, specifically related to Hayling, has been taken furthest by Dr John Creighton, drawing on the evidence of coin imagery as well as the archaeological data.[33] The first temple can be linked with King Commius, possibly as his ancestral shrine or even his own mausoleum/cenotaph. The second temple can be linked with Verica, who revived the site as an ancestral shrine and cult of Commius, in order to legitimate his reign. The succeeding Roman phase was a reinforcement of this cult by the 'Great King of the Britons' Togidubnus.[34]

This interpretation is an important development in the placing of the Hayling Island site in its political and cultural context. It can build on the purely religious attribution of the cult to a Mars-type Celtic deity by the proposal of a linkage between the deity and the Commian dynasty (i.e. it was the dynastic/tribal god). This would suggest that the votive material linked to a Celtic Mars was also part of religious activity associated with ancestral aspects of the Commian (i.e. Atrebatan) dynasty. Such a link would be entirely in keeping with the attributes of tribal protection, warriors and death that are associated with the Celtic Mars.[35]

How was the temple used in practice?

Whatever the actual dedication of the temple, its architecture is clearly designed to enhance the differentiation of the sacred site from the surrounding area. The outer enclosure therefore formed the most significant element of the complex and may have been the *nemeton* in Celtic parlance.[36] The inner enclosure appears to have served primarily as an additional form of differentiation within the enclosure, cutting off what was probably the main ritual area from the rest of the temple. The pit seems to have been the focus.

Deposition, on the other hand, was carried out in specific zones of the site, notably on the south side, i.e. the left-hand side for worshippers approaching the temple and its focus from the entrance on the east side. This zonation may perhaps be linked with allusions by Poseidonius to Celts paying respect to the gods by turning to the right, apparently indicating a spatially significant element to ritual practice, that perhaps also had its counterparts in everyday life.[37] If Poseidonius is taken literally, it could be that sacrificial actions took place on the right-hand (northerly) side of the enclosure, whilst the deposition of the votive remains took place on the left-hand side.

Clearly the act of deposition was important during the making of votive offerings, and for Hayling Island (but not all Iron Age temples, e.g. Gournay) the location of these actions was mainly in a particular south-easterly zone within the enclosure. Interestingly, a south-easterly concentration of artefacts was also detected within the large 7th-5th century BC round-house at Dunston Park, Berkshire. The ritualistic organisation of space on both domestic and ritual sites in southern Britain may have been a powerful aspect of life through much of the Iron Age.

The second temple saw a change in the physical appearance of the site, but the use of space seems to have remained the same, namely an outer enclosure where depositional activity took place, an inner circular enclosure, probably roofed, and a central pit. The significant change was the probable round-house-like building that replaced the inner enclosure. As discussed above, this resembles a domestic structure in plan, and as such, can be regarded as a 'house' for the deity. The motivation for this is not entirely clear: was it a dim reflection of the Graeco-Roman practice of building temples for the gods, or a 'domestication' of the deity arising out of local cultural changes and preferences, or merely the desire to build a shelter for valuable votive offerings that needed to be placed near the ritual focus?[38]

The Roman Temple

The Roman temple had a circular limestone *cella* (shrine structure) with a *pronaos* or porch on its east front (Figs 10 & 11). It was plastered and painted red externally, multi-coloured inside, and roofed with tiles. In the early 2nd century the porch was enlarged. The circular *cella* was built directly over the second Iron Age temple's circular structure, implying clear continuity from the Iron Age phase to its Roman stone successor. The temple was set within a square *temenos* or sacred courtyard, which mirrored the layout of the Iron Age outer enclosure, on a larger scale. Across the *temenos*, a gravel path linked the *cella* to the entrance hall, outer porch and other rooms along the east front of the *temenos*.

The outer porch, like that of the *cella,* was also altered by the addition of foundations along its front. The architectural form of this monumental entrance is not easy to establish but it appears from the archaeological evidence that the rooms may have been divided by columns and access was usually to either side of the central structure. The southern side room contained a black and white mosaic pavement and walls of small limestone blocks in Gallic-style *petit appareil,* both features reminiscent of the nearby 1st-century Fishbourne palace.[39]

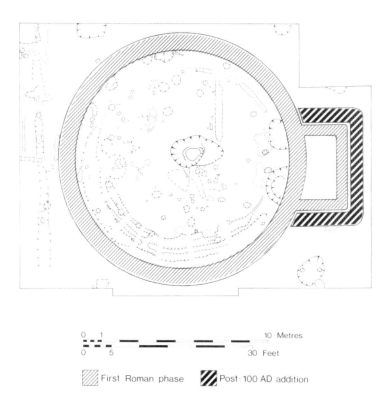

0 1   10 Metres

0   5   30 Feet

First Roman phase   Post-100 AD addition

Fig. 10 The Roman cella *was constructed directly over the second Iron Age temple, as shown here. Its porch was subsequently enlarged early in the 2nd century AD.*

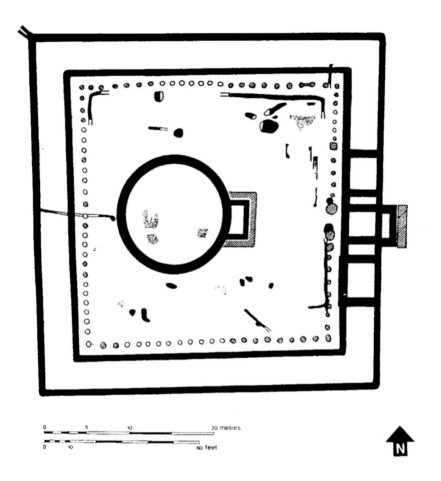

Fig. 11 Plan of the Roman temple.

The rest of the *temenos* consists of a double wall, the outer one solid, the inner one a stylobate (foundation wall) for a colonnade, with the corridor between them gravelled to form an ambulatory or cloister-like arrangement. Around the inner perimeter of the courtyard were two phases of posts, the second dating to the early 2nd century, possibly part of the same building campaign as the porch alterations.[40] Beyond the outer courtyard wall, some 60 m to the north, and 10 m to the east, a ditch and probable wall enclosed a much larger area, probably a boundary to the temple as a whole.

Finds from the Roman Temple

The votive material deposited at the Roman temple is in sharp contrast with that of its Iron Age predecessor. Military equipment and horse and vehicle trappings are absent, perhaps due to the rapid decline of Iron Age 'warrior culture' after the Roman conquest. Civilians were also forbidden from carrying arms, once the new province had been taken into Roman control. Pottery, glass objects, bone pins and animal bones continued to be offered at the temple, together with metal objects, mainly coins and brooches, including enamelled horse and rider and *hippocampus* brooches, the latter a votive object originating in central France (Fig. 12).

Fig. 12 Two enamelled brooches from the Roman temple, depicting a horse-and-rider, and a hippocamp (sea-monster).

A fragmentary inscribed stone altar (Fig. 13) was dedicated by an officer or centurion, possibly named Naevianus, of the *Legio IX Hispana*, which may back up the suggestion made earlier that the temple was dedicated to a local equivalent of Mars.[41] Stone inscriptions are rare from this region of southern Britain, and it raises questions about the presence of this soldier at the temple. Was this an official dedication, or more of a personal vow?

Fig. 13 Part of a stone altar. The upper line has the letters EVIAN, probably for Naevianus or a similar personal name. The lower line has EG, for 'legion', followed by the Roman numeral VIII. In fact this is more likely to be VIIII, as indicated by the superscript line, for the Ninth legion, as this legion is known to be in Britain, rather than the Eighth. The dedication to the god would have been in the lines above the dedicant's name. From the post-packing of a Saxon building in the temple courtyard. Width of stone, 9.5 cm.

The Temple and the Roman Conquest of Britain

Why was such a large and (exceptionally for Britain) early Roman temple built so soon after the conquest? The answer seems to lie in the political alignment of the area at that time. In the late 1st century BC the Commian dynasty had struck up cordial relations with Rome and when, in *c.* AD 25, the Atrebates' northern *oppidum* at *Calleva* (modern Silchester) fell into the (politically anti-Roman) hands of the sons of Cunobelin, King Verica retreated to his southern capital in the Chichester area. Eventually Verica was forced to flee to Rome to appeal to the emperor for help, and in the wake of the invasion the southern Atrebates were allied to Rome.[42]

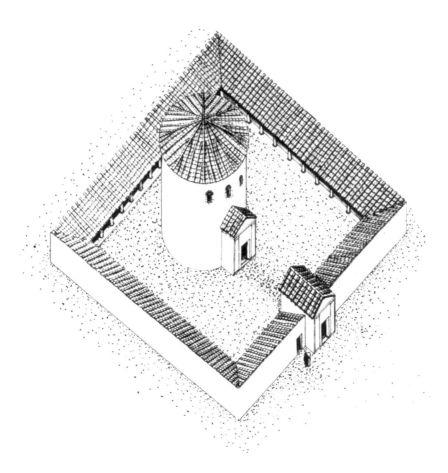

Fig. 14 Reconstuction of the Roman temple in its initial state during the late 1st century AD. Drawing by Robert Downey.

This alliance resulted in the military supply bases at Chichester and Fishbourne serving the Roman invasion and liberation force, particularly Vespasian and the *Legio II Augusta,* in one of their main landfalls and their advance

A Sacred Island

westward into Durotrigian (enemy) territory in AD 43-44. Soon after this in the Neronian and early Flavian period the Iron Age temple was rebuilt in stone on a monumental scale, coinciding with the building of the proto-palace and later Flavian palace at Fishbourne, as well as other structures in the Chichester area. These events can be ascribed to the client king Tiberius Claudius Togidubnus (Cogidubnus), successor to Verica, and it cannot be for-tuitous that Gallic architects and builders seem to have been working on the-se enterprises, perhaps represented by the *collegium fabrorum* (guild of craftsmen) mentioned on Togidubnus's dedicatory inscription from the Chichester temple of Neptune and Minerva.[43] Obviously the Roman emperors were keen to concentrate expertise and expenditure within the area to re-ward Togidubnus for his help during the invasion, to promote 'Romanisation', and also to perpetuate and enhance the native Atrebatic temple at Hayling Island, associated with the southern *oppidum*.

The French (Gallic) Connection

One of the most striking aspects is that the Hayling Island Roman temple is so unlike other 'Romano-Celtic' temples in Britain (Fig. 14), and the search for good parallels leads us to France. The most relevant examples lie in a band across central France with most examples to the west of that area.[44] By con-trast, to the north, east and in Germany the typical double-square temple is almost exclusively found. Four of the largest Hayling Island-type examples are at Périgueux (Dordogne), Cahors (Lot), Talmont (Charente-Maritime) and Sanxay (Vienne).[45] At Périgueux, ancient *Vesunna Petrocoriorum,* the late 1st/early 2nd century temple's *cella* with its surrounding columned ambulatory stands on a podium. Remarkably, the *cella* still stands, 24 m high (Fig. 15), except where the porch was attached on the east side, where it has col-lapsed. The *cella* was originally clad in marble sheeting. Another circular *cella* survives almost intact at La Rigale, Villetoureix (Dordogne). It is smaller than the Hayling Island *cella* with a diameter of 8 m, but stands 10.8 m high and is now incorporated into a chateau which has cut later openings through its originally windowless walls (Fig. 15).[46] It is our best guide to the original ap-pearance of the Roman temple at Hayling Island.

*Fig. 15 Two surviving circular temples in south-west France. The Tour de Ve-
sone, Périgueux (left) and La Rigale, Villetoureix (right).*

Three further Gallo-Roman temples provide more intriguing evidence. Limited excavation has shown that the temple at Entrains had two main phases
of construction, the first probably in the 1st century. The *cella* has no ambulatory, as at Hayling Island and Annoire (Jura).[47] Although the *cella* is compara-
ble in size to Hayling Island's, it lacks a masonry porch; the *temenos* and outer facade, however, appear more grandiose. Another circular temple, at Allonnes (Sarthe), may give a clue to the identity of the cult at Hayling Island,
and there may be some correlation between cult name and plan form in central Gaul. The early votive material deposited at Allonnes is directly similar to
that at Hayling Island and three dedications to Augustus and Mars Mullo
were also set up.[48] The circular temple at Craon (Mayenne), also has a dedication to Mars Mullo, and one cannot help suggesting that the Hayling Island
temple was similarly dedicated.[49] If there is a link between plan-form and a
particular cult-group, then possibly Hayling Island's temple had its origins in a
cult-centre somewhere in western or central France.

A Dynastic Temple, dedicated to Mars?

All this can be supplemented by more recent discoveries and suggestions. These focus upon the excavation of the high-status princely burial, succeeded by a Romano-Celtic temple, at Folly Lane, St Albans, just outside the Iron Age *oppidum* and Roman town of *Verulamium*. This sequence suggests that there were Iron Age temples and their Romano-Celtic successors dedicated to ancestral cults or to deities linked to hero/ancestor worship.[50] This can be related to the Hayling Island temple, in that the first Iron Age phase might be linked with Commius (as discussed earlier), possibly as his ancestral shrine or even his own mausoleum/cenotaph. The second phase might be linked with Verica who revived the site as an ancestral shrine and cult of Commius to legitimate his reign. The succeeding Roman temple was a reinforcement of this cult by Togidubnus.[51] Perhaps a Mars-type Celtic deity was the tribal god of the Commian dynasty, as the Celtic Mars was attributed with tribal protection, warriors and death.

Mars may also have been a suitable deity for expressing loyalty to the Roman state, as one of the major gods in the Roman pantheon.[52] Certainly, most of the large circular temple sites in Gaul were 'official' in nature, often with inscriptions showing loyalty to the emperors. Hayling Island Roman temple may have been similar – a grand rebuilding of the second Iron Age temple, in stone, to demonstrate an affirmation by Verica and Togidubnus of their gratitude for Roman aid and intervention, while at the same time preserving a link back to their Iron Age ancestry at the traditional dynastic temple.

Interlude – decline in the Late Roman period

The Roman temple lasted about 200 years before clear signs of decline became apparent. By the mid-3rd century, masonry had begun to collapse into the courtyard, and the tall *cella* was probably unstable due to lack of maintenance. This coincides with similar signs of abandonment at Fishbourne Palace, where there was a fire, but no subsequent rebuilding. The south coast was becoming unsafe at this time, due to Frankish and Saxon raiding during the 3rd century. Eventually the fort at Portchester was constructed to counter this threat, so that some signs of security in southern Britain had returned by the early 4th century. The Roman temple was not rebuilt, however, and Hayling Island as a whole has very little evidence of late Roman occupation. Interestingly, many 3rd and 4th century coins have been found in the rubble of the collapse of the temple, and they suggest that worshippers may still have been visiting the temple's site, and leaving votive offerings.[53]

Pagan Saxon Revival – a unique ritual site

The excavation of an Anglo-Saxon ritual site and settlement overlying the Iron Age and Roman temple on Hayling Island has perhaps been over-shadowed by the spectacular nature of the Iron Age and Roman evidence. However, the finding of a probable Saxon period ritual site immediately to the south of the earlier temple has raised many questions about the nature of the site in the post-Roman period, and the possibility of some element of continuity or 'sacred memory' of the Roman temple up to the 8th/9th centuries AD.

An indication of Saxon activity in the vicinity of the temple was recorded 100 years ago through Talfourd Ely's fieldwork.[54] This pointed to a cemetery, which was not relocated in the excavations of the 1976-82 and 2001, but the evidence that such a cemetery was found cannot be dismissed, as it may be beyond the area of the excavation and the temple.

The possible Saxon ritual site

Excavations to follow up a geophysical survey took place in 2001,[55] a few metres to the south-west of the Iron Age and Roman temples, and within a large ditched enclosure c. 120 x 100 m, that appears to represent the outer enclosure of the temple site. The magnetometer survey revealed an oval feature c. 25 x 20 m, consisting of a ten strongly positive pit-like anomalies, with a crescent-shaped series of smaller anomalies within (Figs 17 & 18). On excavation, the outer anomalies were found to be pits filled with burnt debris of mid Saxon date, including blocks of limestone similar to the walling of the Roman temple. The pit contents do not suggest that they were 'special deposits' in ritual terms, but the burnt material with the limestone, and a lack of flint building material, suggest a specific selection for the pits.[56] Radiocarbon dates of AD 650-780 and AD 650-900 were obtained from charcoal in two of the pits.[57] The inner anomalies were elongated furnaces, with their bowls facing towards the interior of the oval feature and their flues aligned radially outwards (Fig. 16). The purpose of the furnaces is unclear, but may be associated with preparation of salt or, less probably, lime mortar.[58] The dating and unusual shape of the feature as a whole leads to its tentative interpretation as a setting for pagan Saxon rituals, associated with the nearby small settlement in the ruins of the Roman temple (see below).

Pagan ritual sites of this period are virtually unknown, and the main evidence seems to be simple square or rectangular timber structures, following distantly in the Romano-Celtic tradition.[59] The oval setting of pits and furnaces at Hayling Island appears to be unique. The radiocarbon dates place the Saxon activity at the site in the early Middle Saxon period, and it seems very likely that there was a gap in occupation of some 300 years between the late Roman and mid-Saxon ritual usage of the temple. This points to either a coincidence, or the notion of a memory of the earlier ritual use of the site by the local population in mid-Saxon times.

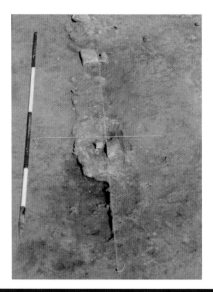

Fig. 16 One of the furnaces in the interior of the possible Saxon oval ritual site. A burnt area in the foreground is overlain by a fire-hardened clay and mortar area in the centre of the photo. A long 'tail' of burnt building debris lies beyond. The purpose of the furnaces is unknown, but may be connected with salt or lime-mortar production.

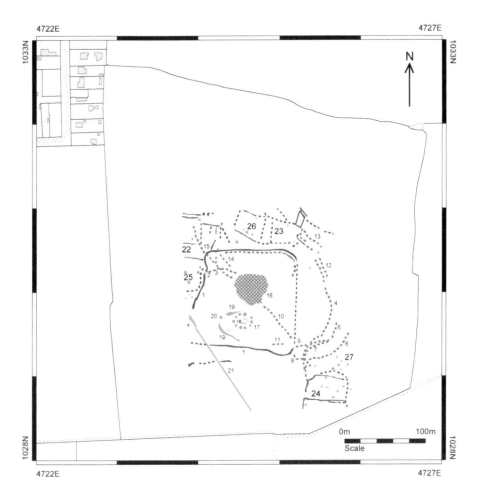

Fig. 17 Interpretation of the magnetometer survey of the temple area in 1999. The Iron Age and Roman temples are no. 16, showing as an amorphous feature after the site had been excavated. The Saxon ritual site is nos. 17 and 18.

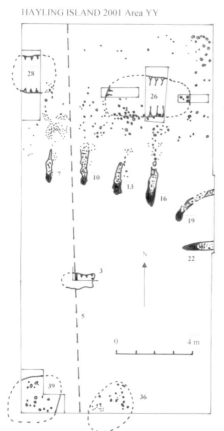

HAYLING ISLAND 2001 Area YY

Fig. 18 Magnetometer plot of the oval Saxon ritual features (below) and excavation plan of the central sector of the Saxon ritual site (left). On the plan, 7, 10, 13, 16, 19 & 22 represent the furnaces in the centre of the site, 26, 28, 36 & 39 are the perimeter pits, and 3 & 5 are 20th century features.

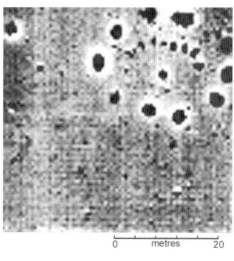

The Saxon ritual site was later than the reintroduction of Christianity to England by St Augustine in AD 597, and can be viewed as valuable indication of the persistence of pagan ideas for some time after the conversion of the South Saxons and the West Saxons in the 7th century AD.[60] The Saxon phase does not appear to have lasted very long, and was presumably given up at the same time as the settlement in the ruins of the Roman temple, in favour of the still-surviving Saxon hamlets of Stoke, Northney and Eastney, where of course, North Hayling church was to be established (see below).

A Sacred Island

The settlement

Within the area of the Roman temple were a series of post-holes, pits and three ditches dug into the rubble of the demolished temple. A further pit was also excavated to the east of the temple courtyard wall. The three ditches lead out from the temple, indicating clearly that the remains of the temple acted as the focus of the settlement, presumably a village. The extent and thickness of Roman building debris must originally been much greater and the Saxon ground surface was disturbed by subsequent robbing of the site for building stone. Robbing of wall foundations was also carried out by the Saxons themselves, particularly on the south side of the *cella*, and the *cella* porch (presumably for stone buildings.), but much other robbing, for instance of the inside *temenos* ambulatory wall, may be of late Roman date. The result of this and subsequent ploughing is that only the lower parts of the excavated features have survived, and many slighter ones have probably long been eroded away.

Some of the least substantial features were a single row of small post holes to the north-west of the *cella*, each packed with reused stone, including the fragment of a Roman limestone inscribed altar, described earlier. Running approximately east-west, these probably represent the incomplete evidence for a fence or a rectangular building, or perhaps even a lean-to structure associated with the *cella* wall, and/or a pit to the south. More evidence of Saxon building comes from the ditch running east from the site, in the form of daub fragments with wattle impressions. The sub-rectangular rubbish-filled cess-pits provide the main evidence of Saxon occupation. Most are in the eastern area of the *temenos* enclosure, with none inside the *cella*, implying that this building survived in some form above ground during this period. The houses associated with this activity presumably lie in a separate area, possibly to the south towards the prevailing wind. Some pits contained coprolites and most had evidence of some cess-pit material. The remains of frogs testify that some pits contained standing water for a period. Two pits contained the remains of structures made from oak planks and one had two shallow stake holes in its bottom. While it is possible that these are the discarded remains of buildings from over, or at least, near the pits, it seems more likely that they are evidence for horizontal-plank linings of cess-pit walls.

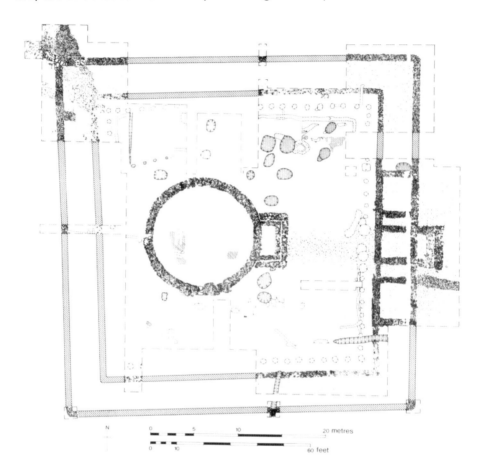

Fig. 19 Outline plan of the Roman temple, with the pits, gullies and other features of the Saxon settlement in grey shading.

After a short time, the pits were used to dispose of food refuse, and similar material was found in the ditches. Much of this survived as marine shells, principally oysters, and also smaller quantities of other species such as winkles and whelks. The evidence indicates a well-organised shell-fishery, the analysis of which has produced some interesting results. The pits also contained the remains of fish, such as plaice, and animal bones, mainly cattle, sheep and pigs. The high proportion of cattle is in stark contrast to the bone assemblages from the Iron Age and Roman levels of the site, where they are virtually absent from the evidence of ritual meals found within the temple *temenos*. Layers of Roman rubble were periodically shovelled into the pits and the best preserved Roman tiles and painted plaster fragments come from these contexts. Finally, most pits were sealed with a cap of natural brick-earth, but in some cases where subsequent substances had occurred, they were revived and then a secondary cap put on top.

Radiocarbon dates from charcoal in the pits gives a range of AD 570-680, slightly earlier than the ritual site.[61]

The features described so far fit well with the cultural and dating evidence from other Solent-coast Saxon sites such as Portchester Castle and Hamwih (Saxon Southampton). There have been excavations which point to probably similar settlements on the coast neighbouring Hayling Island at nearby Emsworth and Rowner. The Saxon pottery from the temple site provides, with the radiocarbon dates, the principal dating evidence for the settlement. Cooking pots, of coarse hand-made ware, and decorated vessels in a laminated dark grey sandy fabric tempered with chalk and flint grits, were found, together with wide-bodied jars, decorated with a horizontal band filled with four-segmented circular stamps below the rim, vertical panels infilled with shallow zig-zag lines, and triangular areas filled with large stamped circles. These interesting forms of pottery are paralleled at Pagham, Portchester, Hamwih and the Old Minster, Winchester and date the occupation to at least the late 8th to 9th century. Interestingly, decorated sherds found on the site by Ely over a century ago, published by Cunliffe, may form part of the vessel recovered during our more recent excavations![62] Other artefactual evidence is very scanty, and is confined to fragments of double-sided bone combs, like the ones well-known from Hamwih.

The Saxon ditches were dug through the ambulatory foundations, showing that the Roman walls must have substantially disappeared by that time, but the fact that the ditches are orientated to the same cardinal axes as the temple suggests that the temple plan and that of its immediate surroundings remained influential in the layout of land divisions in succeeding centuries. The spacing of the ditches make it improbable that they acted as footings of timber buildings; a more likely explanation is that they are fence alignments surrounding building plots. The alternative suggestion that they acted as actual field boundaries seems more improbable, and parallels for this are extremely rare.

We can, however, be more certain about the layout of the open field system around the site, which doubtless had its origins in the late Saxon period. This exhibited a remarkable rectilinear layout with axes related to the cardinal points, which survived more or less intact until the enclosures of the mid-19th century. The possibility of course exists that this layout has its origins in the Roman period, but the more interesting aspect here is that the plan of the temple *temenos* was exactly respected by the layout of individual furlongs. For much of the later medieval period the site lay in the common field belonging to Stoke village, which ran on an exact east-west street alignment to the south of the site. The relationship of the 9th-century Saxon village to Stoke itself is unclear, but the Anglo-Saxon name of the temple site *Tun-sel* or *Tun-stall* has survived in several later forms, of which the commonest is *Towncil* Furlong.[63] This origin could originally have referred to 'hall of the village' (*-sele*), or 'furlongs' (*-selionem*), or to the 'site of the village' (*-stall*). However, the fact that names in *tun* or *town* sometimes referred to the decayed sites of large Roman buildings should not be overlooked. It is interesting that the hamlets of Northney, Eastney and Westney, of late Saxon origin, seem to cluster closely along the north-south alignment due east of the site and these, together with Stoke, became the established foci of medieval settlement after the Norman conquest, when Towncil was deserted to be replaced by an arable field.

A thriving agricultural and livestock based economy is explicit in the archaeological evidence from the site, together with well-organised exploitation of the marine fisheries. After the village's desertion, for reasons which remain unclear, this situation, together with salt panning, continued to exist on Hayling Island generally, as is recorded in the Domesday survey.[64]

Saxon Hayling Island

Other documented data for the development of Saxon settlement on the on the island is limited. We do know, however, that before the Norman conquest there were, in addition to royal connections, close links with St Swithun's Priory at the Old Minster, Winchester. This situation is closely paralleled at Saxon Portchester where it is suggested that the Winchester connection might imply the existence of an early church founded within the Roman defences, and a Saxon stone tower, surrounded by a coeval cemetery, has indeed been excavated there. At Hayling Island, any cemetery belonging to the excavated settlement will also have belonged to a church. There is however, no archaeological evidence to the existence of a Saxon church close to the site, but further south a decorated sculpted stone base from a Saxon standing cross was found about 150 years ago. This can be dated on stylistic grounds to the 9th century. Also it is very likely that the old church of All Saints, lost in the encroachments of the sea by the 13th century, was of Saxon origin. It was this church, and indeed much of the island that William the Conqueror granted to Jumièges Abbey so they could administer the local economy through an alien priory. The church of St. Peter, due east of the site in Eastney, betrays no evidence of Saxon origin, although this has sometimes been assumed perhaps on the basis of its being built on erratic sarsens, possibly robbed from the temple's foundations. Its existing fabric is generally agreed to be post-conquest. This has always been a chapel-of-ease to the medieval parish and priory church of the whole island, dedicated to St Mary the Virgin, built *de novo* two miles to the south by Jumièges in the mid 13th century.[65]

Notes

[1] This is fully discussed in Allen & Gardiner's important archaeological and environmental study (2000) of the Langstone Harbour area.

[2] Bradley 1975.

[3] Earlier excavations had taken place prior to the 1st World War, directed by Dr Talfourd Ely, of University College London (Ely 1908). He considered the site to be a villa, of an unusual plan, rather than a temple. M J T Lewis (1966) was the first person to suggest in print that it might be a temple site.

[4] The distance between the east and west sides of the enclosure is 8.60 m, which may conform to 28 units of a module (a 'foot') of 307 mm. This is close to the modules of 310 mm at Manching, Bavaria, and 304.2 mm at Mont Beuvray, central France (Schubert & Schubert 1993; Schubert 1994), and may indicate use of a metrical unit in laying out the enclosure. Subsidiary measurements of the inner enclosure suggest that the module was used for some of the details of the layout (further analysis of which is proceeding). The inner enclosure was also probably laid out so that the east-west to north-south ratio was c. 4:5.

[5] 410-110 cal BC at one sigma, and 760 cal BC – cal AD 50 at two sigma (HAR-8533). See Bayliss et al. 2012, 142-3. The two-sigma date is contemporary with the artefactual evidence, but the one-sigma date of up to 110 BC is at the earliest limit of the other dating evidence.

[6] Cal AD 20-210 (HAR-8534) for the pit; cal AD 60-330 (HAR-8535) for the linked feature.

[7] For instance at Vieux-Poitiers (Lejeune 1988, 70-82) and in Armorica (ancient Brittany) in probable funerary contexts (Daire & Villard 1996). For the Hampshire sarsen survey, see Gallup 1994. For Triguères, see Horne & King 1980, 482-3.

[8] A full report on the Iron Age and Roman coins, by Daphne Briggs, Colin Haselgrove and Cathy King, is in Briggs et al. 1993. See also Haselgrove 1987, 129-30; 2005; De Jersey 1999.

[9] This bit, of Palk's 'double-jointed snaffle' category (Palk 1984, DJ17), has its most notable parallels from the Lady's Barrow and King's Barrow, Arras, Yorkshire (Stead 1979), Hengistbury Head, Dorset (Palk 1987, 151-2), Otterbourne, Hants (Denford 1993, 39-41) and elsewhere. The last-mentioned site is only a short distance from Hayling Island.

[10] It has knob decoration of Arras type (Leeds 1933, type I).

[11] Illustrated in King & Soffe 1998, Fig. 2. Mont-Beuvray examples: Goudineau & Peyre 1993, 115-7.

[12] The linch-pins are paralleled at Worthy Down, Hampshire (Dunning et al. 1929) and Llyn Cerrig Bach, Anglesey (Fox 1946). For the Champagne and Arras burials, see Stead 1979.

[13] Owslebury warrior burial: Collis 1973. Ritual bronze rings: Bailey & Woodward 1993, 135-40.

[14] Woodward 1992, 66-7; Lejars 1996; King 2007a.

[15] The spearheads are similar to examples from the hillforts of Hod Hill, Dorset (Brailsford 1962), Maiden Castle, Dorset (Wheeler 1943) and Danebury, Hants (Cunliffe 1984, 361-6). Gournay shield binding: Brunaux & Rapin 1988, 223). Recent finds have clearly demonstrated the purpose of this type of binding was for shields rather than sword scabbards (Stead 1991a).

[16] Yorkshire vehicle burials: Stead 1991b; Folly Lane: Niblett 1999.

[17] As at St-Aubin-sur-Gaillon, northern France (Poulain 1913; Horne & King 1980, 457-8), Ivy Chimneys, Witham, Essex (Turner & Wymer 1987) and on other types of Roman site (Adkins & Adkins 1985; Bradley 1986).

[18] Gournay: Brunaux et al. 1985; Ribemont: Cadoux 1982; Brunaux et al. 1999. Fesques: Mantel 1997. Miranda Aldhouse Green (2001) discusses the evidence for human sacrifice.

[19] The percentages at Hayling are sheep 59%, pig 41%, (n = 2395): see King 2005. Uley: Levitan 1993.

[20] Briggs et al.1992, catalogue nos 143-8. Bean 2000, 253-62, 272-3. See also King 2008 for discussion of zonation at Hayling and other temple sites.

[21] For further discussion of brooch deposition at Hayling, see Haselgrove 1997.

[22] Webster 1986, 132. For the coins: De Jersey 2005; Kiernan 2001; Briggs *et al.* 1993, 2-3.

[23] As reflected in Caesar's reference (*BG* 6.13) to the heaps of spoils in the territory of the Carnutes.

[24] Brunaux & Malagoli (2003) review the evidence for Iron Age temple sites in northern France.

[25] Caesar *BG* 8.48; Frontinus, *Strat.* 2.13.11; Hawkes 1977, 184, map 12; Trott & Tomalin 2003, 176.

[26] Cunliffe 1991, 108-10.

[27] See further discussion of this in King 1990 and 2007b.

[28] Strabo 4.4.6; Pomponius Mela 3.6.8; Tacitus *Annals* 14.30; Webster 1995, 451. The evidence for Hayling being an island, or at the very least, a dry 'island' in a vast area of salt-marsh, is discussed by Allen and Gardiner (2000, 214-7).

[29] Bedwin 1984, 50-1; Aldsworth 1987; Manley 2008, 43-5.

[30] Downey *et al.* 1980, 300.

[31] Niblett 1999.

[32] King & Soffe 1994, 34; Forcey 1998.

[33] Creighton 2000, 192-7.

[34] As his title is given on the Chichester inscription, RIB 1.92. See also Henig 2002.

[35] Thevenot 1968, 53-6; Green 1986, 103-10.

[36] Piggott 1978; see also Webster 1995.

[37] Poseidonius' text does not survive, but is quoted by Athenaeus (4.152D). See also Webster 1995, 460; Fitzpatrick 1994; 1997.

[38] Fauduet 2010, 144-51; King 1990, 223; 2007b.

[39] Cunliffe 1971, pl. 12. A useful comparison can be made with the very similar temple at Entrains, Nièvre, central France (Meissonnier 1985; Fauduet 2010, 112-13; Goguey, pers. comm.) which has side entrances only, with a large monumental niche occupying the central position, originally plastered but later faced with marble.

[40] A similar courtyard arrangement is known at the large temple at le Moulin-du-Fâ (or Barzan), Talmont, Charente-Maritime (Aupert 2010).

[41] *Britannia* 12, 1981, 369; RIB III.3042.

[42] Creighton 2000, 218-21.

[43] RIB I.92.

[44] Horne & King 1980; Table-ronde 2004.

[45] Périgueux: Lauffray 1990; Cahors: Fauduet 2002, 24; Rigal in Table-ronde 2004; Talmont: Aupert 2010; Sanxay: Aupert 1992.

[46] Horne & King 1980, entry for Villetoureix.

[47] Entrains: Meissonnier 1985; Annoire: Jeannin & Chouquer 1978.

[48] Brouquier-Reddé & Gruel 2004; Brouquier-Reddé *et al.* 2006; ILTG 343-345; Térouanne 1960.

[49] CIL 13.3096; Térouanne 1960; De Bodard 1863. Temples to Mars in the north-west Roman provinces are discussed in the papers in Brouquier-Reddé *et al.* 2006.

[50] Niblett 1999. For burials next to the temple at Lancing, Sussex: Bedwin 1981; Rudling 2008, 111-14.

[51] See Creighton 2000, 191-7; Haselgrove 2005, 399-400.

[52] Christopher Smith discusses this aspect of Mars in his review of Brouquier-Reddé *et al.* 2006, in *Bryn Mawr Classical Review*, 2007, 02.20, online publication. See also Marco Simón 2011, 145.

[53] Many temples in Gaul were also abandoned in the 3rd century (Goodman 2011, 170-1), but few have evidence for visits to the site after abandonment.

[54] Ely 1908.

[55] The geophysical survey was undertaken in 1999 by Richard McConnell (Context One Archaeology) and Alex Turner (University of Winchester).

[56] See Hamerow (2006) for discussion of 'special deposits' in pagan Anglo-Saxon archaeology.

[57] Cal AD 650-780 at 1 sigma (Wk-10542); cal AD 650-900 at 1 sigma (Wk-10543).

[58] The importance of salt in the local economy during the Iron Age and Roman period is well-known (Bradley 1975; Allen & Gardiner 2000, 214-7), but the evidence for the Saxon period is virtually non-existent. It is likely, however, to have been an important aspect of mid-Saxon coastal settlement.

[59] Blair 1995. See also Semple 2011.

[60] There is no evidence that the site was Christianised, unlike a number of other Roman temple sites; see Dierkens 1998, 41-3; Goodman 2011, 181-6.

[61] Cal AD 570-680 (HAR-8532); cal AD 540-670 (HAR-8536); cal AD 220-430 (HAR-8537); see Bayliss *et al.* 2012, 142-3. The last date probably relates to charcoal of the late Roman period redeposited in one of the Saxon pits.

[62] Cunliffe 1974, Fig. 1.

[63] Coates 2007, 41-2.

[64] See Keen 1988.

[65] Soffe 1995.

References in the Notes

Adkins, L & Adkins, R 1985: Neolithic axes from Roman sites in Britain. *Oxford Journal of Archaeology* 4, 69-75.

Aldhouse Green, M 2001: *Dying for the Gods. Human sacrifice in Iron Age and Roman Europe.* Stroud, Tempus.

Aldsworth, F G 1987: Prehistoric and Roman Selsey. *Sussex Archaeological Collections* 125, 41-50.

Allen, M J & Gardiner, J 2000: *Our Changing Coast: a survey of the intertidal archaeology of Langstone Harbour, Hampshire.* York, Council for British Archaeology Research Report 124.

Aupert, P 1992: *Sanxay. Un grand sanctuaire rural gallo-romain.* Paris: Imprimerie nationale.

Aupert, P 2010: *Barzan II. Le Sanctuaire au temple circulaire ("Moulin-du-Fâ"): tradition celtique et influences gréco-romaines.* Bordeaux, Aquitania Supplément 22.

Bailey, J & Woodward, A 1993: Rings. In Woodward & Leach 1993, 135-40.

Bayliss, A *et al.* 2012: *Radiocarbon Dates from samples funded by English Heritage between 1981 and 1988.* Swindon, English Heritage.

Bean, S C 2000: *The Coinage of the Atrebates and Regni.* Oxford, Oxford University School of Archaeology Monograph 50.

Bedwin, O 1981: Excavations at Lancing Down, West Sussex, 1980. *Sussex Archaeological Collections* 119, 37-56.

Bedwin, O 1984: Aspects of Iron Age settlement in Sussex. In Cunliffe, B W & Miles, D (eds), *Aspects of the Iron Age in Central Southern Britain.* Oxford, Oxford University Committee for Archaeology Monograph 2, 46-51.

Blair, J 1995: Anglo-Saxon pagan shrines and their prototypes. *Anglo-Saxon Studies in Archaeology & History* 8, 1-28.

Bradley, R 1975: Salt and settlement in the Hampshire-Sussex borderland. In Brisay, K de & Evans, K (eds.), *Salt. The study of an ancient industry.* Colchester, Colchester Archaeology Group, 20-5.

Bradley, R 1986: Neolithic axes in Roman Britain: an exercise in archaeological source criticism. *Oxford Journal of Archaeology* 5, 119-20.

Brailsford, J W 1962: *Hod Hill I.* London, British Museum.

A Sacred Island

Briggs, D, Haselgrove, C & King, C 1993: Iron Age and Roman coins from Hayling Island temple. *British Numismatic Journal* 62, 1-62.

Brouquier-Reddé, V & Gruel, K 2004: Le sanctuaire de *Mars Mullo* chez les Aulerques Cénomans (Allonnes, Sarthe) Ve s. av. J-C – IVe s. apr. J-C: état des recherches actuelles. *Gallia* 61, 291-396.

Brouquier-Reddé, V, *et al.* 2006: (eds.) *Mars en Occident*. Rennes, Presses Universitaires de Rennes.

Brunaux, J-L & Malagoli, C 2003: La France du Nord. Pp. 9-73 in Cultes et sanctuaires en France à l'Âge du Fer. *Gallia* 60, 1-268.

Brunaux, J-L, Meniel, P & Poplin, F 1985: *Gournay I. Les fouilles sur le sanctuaire et l'oppidum (1975-1984)*, Amiens, Revue Archéologique de Picardie, numéro spécial.

Bruneaux, J-L & Rapin, A 1988: *Gournay II, Boucliers et lances, dépôts et trophées*. Amiens, Revue Archéologique de Picardie, numéro spécial.

Brunaux, J-L *et al.* 1999: Ribemont-sur-Ancre (Somme). Bilan préliminaire et nouvelles hypothèses. *Gallia* 56, 177-283.

Cadoux, J L 1982: L'ossuaire gaulois de Ribemont-sur-Ancre (Somme). *Revue Archéologique de Picardie* 1982, 3, 12-13.

CIL = *Corpus Inscriptionum Latinarum*, Berlin: vol. XIII, Gallia, 1899-1916.

Coates, R 2007: *The Place-Names of Hayling Island, Hampshire*. Manuscript of 1991, revised 2007 and available electronically via University of the West of England website.

Collis, J 1973: Burials with weapons in Iron Age Britain. *Germania* 51, 121-33.

Creighton, J 2000: *Coins and Power in Late Iron Age Britain*. Cambridge, Cambridge University Press.

Cunliffe, B W 1971: *Excavations at Fishbourne 1961-1969, vol. 1, the site*. London, Report of the Research Committee of the Society of Antiquaries of London 26.

Cunliffe, B W 1974: Some late Saxon stamped pottery from southern England. In Evison, V *et al.* 1974 (eds.), *Medieval Pottery from Excavations. Studies presented to Gerald Clough Dunning, with a bibliography of his works*. London, J Baker, 127-35.

Cunliffe, B W 1984: *Danebury, an Iron Age Hillfort in Hampshire, II, the excavations 1969-1978, the finds*. London, Council for British Archaeology.

Cunliffe, B W 1991: *Iron Age Communities in Britain* (3rd ed.). London, Routledge.

Daire, M-Y & Villard, A 1996: Les stèles de l'Age du Fer à décors géométriques et curvilignes. Etat de la question dans l'ouest armoricain. *Revue Archéologique de l'Ouest* 13, 123-56.

De Bodard, [M] 1863: Antiquités des environs de Craon. *Mémoires de la Société académique de Maine et Loire* 13, 85-93.

De Jersey, P 1999: Exotic Celtic coinage in Britain. *Oxford Journal of Archaeology* 18, 189-216.

De Jersey, P 2005: Deliberate defacement of British Iron Age coinage. In Haselgrove, C & Wigg-Wolf, D (eds.), *Iron Age Coinage and Ritual Practices*. Mainz, Studien zu Fundmünzen der Antike 20, 85-113.

Denford, G T 1993: Some exotic discoveries at Silkstead Sandpit, Otterbourne, and the possible site of an ancient temple. *Proceedings of the Hampshire Field Club & Archaeological Society* 48, 27-54.

Dierkens, A 1998: The evidence of archaeology. In Milis, L (ed.), *The Pagan Middle Ages*. Woodbridge, The Boydell Press, 39-64.

Downey, R, King, A & Soffe, G 1980: The Hayling Island temple and religious connections across the Channel. In Rodwell 1980, 289-304.

Dunning, G C, Hooley, W & Tildesley, M L 1929: Excavations of an Early Iron Age village on Worthy Down, Winchester. *Proceedings of the Hampshire Field Club & Archaeological Society* 10, 178-92.

Ely, T. 1908: *Roman Hayling: a contribution to the history of Roman Britain* (2nd ed.). London, Taylor and Francis.

Fauduet, I 2002: Les sanctuaires gallo-romains, quoi de neuf? *L'Archéologue* 61, 22-6.

Fauduet, I 2010: *Les Temples de Tradition celtique en Gaule romaine*. 2nd ed., Paris, Errance.

Fitzpatrick, A P 1994: Outside in: the structure of an Early Iron Age house at Dunston Park, Thatcham, Berkshire. In Fitzpatrick, A P & Morris, E L (eds.), *The Iron Age in Wessex: recent work*. Salisbury, Trust for Wessex Archaeology, 68-72.

Fitzpatrick, A P 1997: Everyday life in Iron Age Wessex. In Gwilt & Haselgrove 1997, 73-86.

Forcey, C 1998: Whatever happened to the heroes? Ancestral cults and the enigma of Romano-Celtic temples. In Forcey, C, *et al.* (eds) *TRAC 1997. Proceedings of the seventh Annual Theoretical Roman Archaeology Conference Leicester 1997*. Oxford, Oxbow Books, 1-14.

Fox, C 1946: *A Find of the Early Iron Age from Llyn Cerrig Bach, Anglesey*. Cardiff, National Museum of Wales.

Gallup, P 1994: The survey of sarsen stones — Hampshire. *Hampshire Field Club & Archaeological Society, Section Newsletters* 2nd ser., 22, 11-13.

Goodman, P J 2011: Temples in Late Antique Gaul. In Lavan, L & Mulryan, M (eds.), *The Archaeology of Late Antique 'Paganism'*. Leiden, Brill, 165-93.

Goudineau, C & Peyre, C 1993: *Bibracte et les Eduens: à la découverte d'un peuple gaulois*. Paris, Editions Errance.

Green, M J 1986: *The Gods of the Celts*. Gloucester, Alan Sutton.

Gwilt, A & Haselgrove, C 1997: (eds.) *Reconstructing Iron Age Societies*. Oxford, Oxbow Monograph 71.

Hamerow, H 2006: 'Special deposits' in Anglo-Saxon settlements. *Medieval Archaeology* 50, 1-30.

Haselgrove, C 1987: *Iron Age Coinage in South-East England: the archaeological context*. Oxford, British Archaeological Reports British Series 174.

Haselgrove, C 1997: Iron Age brooch deposition and chronology. In Gwilt & Haselgrove 1997, 51-72.

Haselgrove, C 2005: A trio of temples: a reassessment of Iron Age coin deposition at Hayling Island, Harlow and Wanborough. In Haselgrove, C & Wigg-Wolf, D (ed.), *Iron Age Coinage and Ritual Practices*. Mainz, Studien zu Fundmünzen der Antike 20, 381-418.

Hawkes, C F C 1977: Britain and Julius Caesar. *Proceedings of the British Academy* 63, 125-92.

Henig, M 2002: *The Heirs of King Verica. Culture and Politics in Roman Britain*. Stroud, The History Press.

Horne, P & King, A 1980: Romano-Celtic temples in Continental Europe: a gazetteer of those with known plans. In Rodwell 1980, 369-555.

ILTG = *Inscriptions Latines des Trois Gaules*, Paris, Gallia Supplément 17, 1963.

Jeannin, N & Chouquer, G 1978: Eléments pour une géographie historique du Finage (Jura) à l'époque gallo-romaine. *Revue Archéologique de l'Est* 29, 267-302.

Keen, L 1988: Coastal salt production in Norman England. *Anglo-Norman Studies* 11, 133-79.

Kiernan, P 2001: The ritual mutilation of coins on Romano-British sites. *British Numismatic Journal* 71, 18-33.

King, A C 1990: The emergence of Romano-Celtic religion. In Blagg, T and Millett M. (eds.), *The Early Roman Empire in the West*. Oxford, Oxbow, 220-41.

King, A C 2005: Animal remains from temples in Roman Britain. *Britannia* 36, 329-70.

King, A C 2007a: Characterizing assemblages of votive offerings at Romano-Celtic temples in Britain. In Hainzmann, M (ed.), *Auf den Spuren keltischer Götterverehung. Akten des 5. F.E.R.C.AN.-Workshop, Graz, 9-12 October 2003*, Vienna, Verlag der Österreichischen Akademie der Wissenschaften, 183-96.

King, A C 2007b: Romano-Celtic temples in Britain: Gallic influence or indigenous development? In Haeussler, R, & King, A C (eds.), *Continuity and Innovation in Religion in the Roman West, volume 1*. Portsmouth, RI, Journal of Roman Archaeology, Supplementary Series 67, 13-18.

King, A C 2008: Coins and coin hoards from Romano-Celtic temples in Britain. In Haeussler, R, & King, A C (eds.), *Continuity and Innovation in Religion in the Roman West, volume 2*. Portsmouth, RI, Journal of Roman Archaeology, Supplementary Series 67, 25-42.

King, A & Soffe, G 1994: Recherches récentes sur les temples romano-celtique de Grande-Bretagne. L'exemple de Hayling Island. In Goudineau, C, Fauduet, I & Coulon, G (ed.), *Les Sanctuaires de Tradition Indigène en Gaule Romaine*. Paris, Editions Errance, Musée d'Argentomagus, 33-48.

King, A & Soffe, G 1998: Internal organisation and deposition at the Iron Age temple on Hayling Island. *Proceedings of the Hampshire Field Club & Archaeological Society (Hampshire Studies 1998)* 53, 35-47.

Lauffray, J 1990: *La Tour de Vésone à Périgueux. Temple de Vesunna Petrucoriorum*, Paris, Gallia Supplément 49.

Leeds, E T 1933: *Celtic Ornament in the British Isles down to AD 700*. Oxford, Clarendon Press.

Lejars, T 1996: Les armes en fer: une source d'information privilégiée pour l'étude du fonctionnement des sanctuaires celtiques. *Mélanges d'Ecole Française de Rome, Antiquité* 108, 607-30.

Lejeune, M 1988: *Recueil des Inscriptions Gauloises (RIG), volume II, fasc. 1, Textes gallo-étrusques, textes gallo-latines sur pierre*. Paris, Gallia Supplément 45.

Levitan, B 1993: Vertebrate remains. In Woodward & Leach 1993, 257-301.

Lewis, M J T 1966: *Temples in Roman Britain*. Cambridge, Cambridge University Press.

Manley, J 2008: (ed.) *The Archaeology of Fishbourne and Chichester. A framework for its future.* Lewes, Sussex Archaeological Society.

Mantel, E 1997: (ed.) *Le Sanctuaire de Fesques, 'Le Mont du Val aux Moines', Seine Maritime*. Berck-sur-Mer, Nord-Ouest Archéologie 8.

Marco Simón, F 2011: Roman policy regarding native and provincial cults in the west (2nd c. BC-2nd c. AD). In Cecconi, G & Gabrielli, C (eds.), *Politiche religiose nel Mondo antico e Tardoantico*. Bari, Edipuglia, 135-46.

Meissonnier, J 1985: 58 Entrains-sur-Nohain, Sanctuaire du Moulin Vent, 1985, rapport de sondages. Groupe de Recherches archéologiques d'Entrains (Nièvre), unpublished report.

Niblett, R 1999: *The Excavation of a Ceremonial Site at Folly Lane, Verulamium*. London, Britannia Monograph 14.

Palk, N A 1984: *Iron Age Bridle Bits from Britain*. Edinburgh, Edinburgh University Department of Archaeology.

Palk, N A 1987: Bridle bit. In Cunliffe, B W, *Hengistbury Head, Dorset, I: the prehistoric and Roman settlement, 3500 BC-AD 500*. Oxford, Oxford University Committee for Archaeology Monograph 13, 151-2.

Piggott, S 1978: Nemeton, temenos bothros: sanctuaries of the ancient Celts. In Accademia Nazionale dei Lincei (ed.) *I Celti e la loro Cultura nell'Epoca Pre-Romana e Romana nella Britannia*. Rome, Accademia Nazionale dei Lincei.

Poulain, G 1913: Les fana ou temples gallo-romaines de St-Aubin-sur-Gaillon (Eure). *Bulletin de la Société Normande d'Etudes Préhistoriques* 21, 48-82.

RIB = *The Roman Inscriptions of Britain, vol. I, inscriptions on stone*. Oxford, Clarendon Press, 1965; *vol. III, inscriptions on stone*. Oxford, Oxbow Books, 2009.

Rodwell, W (ed.) 1980: *Temples, Churches and Religion: recent research in Roman Britain*. Oxford, British Archaeological Reports British Series 77.

Rudling, D 2008: Roman-period temples, shrines and religion in Sussex. In Rudling, D (ed.), *Ritual Landscapes of Roman South-East Britain*. Oxford: Oxbow Books, 95-137.

Schubert, F 1994: Zur Mass- und Entwurfslehre keltischer Holzbauten im Oppidum von Manching. *Germania* 72/1, 133-92.

Schubert, F. & Schubert, M 1993: Metrological research into the foot measurement found in the Celtic oppidum of Manching. *Complutum* 4, 227-36.

Semple, S 2011: Sacred spaces and places in pre-Christian and conversion period Anglo-Saxon England. In Hamerow, H *et al.* (eds.), *Oxford Handbook of Anglo-Saxon England.* Oxford, Oxford University Press, 742-63.

Soffe, G 1995: *The Priory and Parish Church of St Mary the Virgin Hayling Island*, Hayling Island.

Stead, I M 1979: *The Arras Culture*. York, The Yorkshire Philosophical Society

Stead, I M 1991a: Many more Iron Age shields from Britain. *Antiquaries Journal* 71, 1-35.

Stead, I M 1991b: *Iron Age Cemeteries in East Yorkshire. Excavations at Burton Fleming, Rudston, Garton-on-the-Wolds and Kirkburn.* Swindon, English Heritage.

Table-ronde 2004: *Table-ronde sur les temples circulaires*, Bordeaux, Maison de l'archéologie, 23 Novembre 2002, published in *Aquitania* 20, 2004.

Térouanne, P 1960: Dédicaces à Mars Mullo découvertes à Allonnes (Sarthe). *Gallia* 18, 185-9.

Thevenot, E 1968: *Divinités et Sanctuaires de la Gaule.* Paris, Fayard.

Trott, K & Tomalin, D 2003: The maritime role of the island of Vectis in the British pre-Roman Iron Age. *International Journal of Nautical Archaeology* 32, 158-81.

Turner, R, & Wymer, J J 1987: An assemblage of Palaeolithic hand-axes from the Roman religious complex at Ivy Chimneys, Witham, Essex. *Antiquaries Journal* 67, 43-60.

Webster, G 1986: *The British Celts and their Gods under Rome.* London, Batsford.

Webster, J 1995: Sanctuaries and sacred places. In Green, M J (ed.), *The Celtic World.* London, Routledge, 445-64.

Wheeler, R E M 1943: *Maiden Castle, Dorset.* London, Society of Antiquaries.

Woodward, A 1992: *Shrines and Sacrifice*. London, Batsford.

Woodward, A & Leach, P 1993: *The Uley Shrines: excavation of a ritual complex on West Hill, Uley, Gloucestershire, 1977-9.* London, English Heritage.

Uncovering votive deposits of bones and pottery in the temple courtyard, 1978

Photographing Saxon ritual furnaces, 2001

Further Reading

Abbreviation: HI = Hayling Island

Publications of the site before it was recognized as a temple:

Ely, T 1898 'The antiquities of Hayling Island', *Archaeological Journal* 55, 286-95. [First account of Ely's initial excavations in 1897 and the research which led up to them, including an account of the discoveries of H R Trigg and W Carpenter Turner (c. 1878-96)]

Ely, T 1904 *Roman Hayling: A Contribution to the History of Roman Britain*, London. [Ely's first interim report on his excavations from 1897 onwards and published version of dissertation accepted (London University) for degree of DLitt, 1903; site interpreted as a 'villa']

Ely, T 1908 *Roman Hayling: A Contribution to the History of Roman Britain*, London, 2nd and enlarged ed. with two plans and illus. [Second and final report on Ely's excavations, includes those carried out 1904-1907]

Haverfield, F 1900 'Romano-British Hampshire', in *Victoria County History of Hampshire*, vol. 1, 265-349. [The list of sites has the HI site as no. 36 (p. 310); Ely's current excavations reported on and site described as a possible 'villa']

Lewis, M J T 1966 *Temples in Roman Britain*, Cambridge U P. [On the basis of Ely's work, Lewis suggests 'perhaps temple...but could be mausoleum...' pp. 85-86, plan fig. 90, p. 189 shown at wrong scale]

Scott, R 1826 *A Topographical and Historical Account of Hayling Island, Hants*, Havant. [Published anonymously, first mention of the site; contains remarkably early description of the crop-mark of the Roman masonry temple buildings, pp. 94-97]

Publications of the temple excavations and finds:

Briggs, D, Haselgrove, C & King, C 1993 'Iron Age and Roman coins from the Hayling Island temple', *British Numismatic Journal* 1992, 1-62, pls. 1-7.

Downey, R, King, A & Soffe G 1977 'Cropmarks and air photographs of the Roman temple, Hayling Island, Hants', *Aerial Archaeology* 1, 13-15.

Downey, R, King, A & Soffe G 1978 'The Roman temple on Hayling Island', *Current Archaeololgy* 62, (vol. VI, no.3), 83-7.

Downey, R, King, A & Soffe G 1979 *The Hayling Island Temple, Third Interim Report on the Excavation of the Iron Age and Roman Temple 1976-78*, London, Hayling Island Excavation Project.

Downey, R, King, A & Soffe G 1980 'The Hayling Island temple and religious connections across the Channel', in Rodwell W (ed.), *Temples, Churches and Religion: Recent Research in Roman Britain with a Gazetteer of Romano-Celtic Temples in Continental Europe*, Oxford, British Archaeological Reports British Series, 77 (i), 289-304.

King, A & Soffe, G 1991 'Hayling Island', in Jones, R F J (ed.) *Britain in the Roman Period: recent trends*, Sheffield, J R Collis Publications, 111-13.

A Sacred Island

King, A & Soffe, G 1994 'The Iron Age and Roman temple on Hayling Island, Hampshire', in Fitzpatrick, A P and Morris, E L (ed.), *The Iron Age in Wessex: recent work*, Salisbury, Association Française d'Etude de L'Age du Fer and Trust for Wessex Archaeology, 114-16.

King, A & Soffe, G 1994 'Recherches récentes sur les temples romano-celtiques de Grande-Bretagne, L'exemple de Hayling Island', in Goudineau, C, Fauduet, I & Coulon, G (ed.), *Les Sanctuaires de Tradition Indigène en Gaule Romaine*, Paris, Editions Errance, Musée d'Argentomagus, 33-48.

King, A & Soffe, G 1998 'Internal organisation and deposition at the Iron Age temple on Hayling Island', *Proceedings of the Hampshire Field Club & Archaeological Society (Hampshire Studies 1998)* 53, 35-47.

King, A & Soffe, G 2008 'Hayling Island: a Gallo-Roman temple in Britain', in Rudling, D (ed.), *Ritual Landscapes of Roman South-East Britain*, Great Dunham and Oxford: Heritage Marketing and Publications and Oxbow Books, 139-44.

King, A & Soffe, G 2008 'A bibliography of the Iron Age and Roman temple on Hayling Island', in *ibidem*, 144-51.

Palk, B 1984 *Iron Age Bridle Bits from Britain*, Edinburgh University Occasional Papers 10. [for bridle bits from HI temple]

Pitts, M (in conjunction with King, A & Soffe, G) 2001 'Hayling Island. The Iron Age and Roman temple site on the Hampshire coast continues to surprise', *Current Archaeology* 176, 333-5. [Interim report on the 2001 excavations].

Soffe, G 1995 *The Priory and Parish Church of St Mary the Virgin Hayling Island*, Alresford, Applegraphics Ltd. [pp 47-50: discussion on reused building stones]

Taylor, R & Brailsford, J V 1985 'British Iron Age strap-unions', *Proceedings of the Prehistoric Society* 51, 247-72. [for strap-unions from the HI temple]

Tomlin, R S O, Wright, R P & Hassall, M W 2009 'Hayling Island (Hants.)', *Roman Inscriptions of Britain, vol III, inscriptions on stone,* Oxford, Oxbow Books, 56. [for the inscription, RIB 3042]

Interim notes:

Britannia 8, 1977, 418; 9, 1978, 463-4, plan fig. 18; 10, 1979, 329-31; 11, 1980, 393; 12, 1981, 361; 369 (inscription); 13, 1982, 389; 15, 1984, 324

Hampshire Field Club & Archaeological Society, Archaeology Section Newsletter 1, no. 3, 1982, 8-11; 1, no. 5, 1983, 2-12